# THE
# BOOK OF SIMON

By
## A. S. M. HUTCHINSON

*With Illustrations by*
A. H. WATSON

BOSTON    1930

## LITTLE, BROWN, AND COMPANY

To
SIMON
from his
AFFECTIONATE PARENTS
HOPING THAT
WHEN HE IS OLD ENOUGH
TO READ IT
He will not
UPBRAID HIS FATHER
for having
WRITTEN IT

# CONTENTS

## I

*The Astounding Life of My Son*  1

## II

*The Astounding Advancement of My Son*  19

## III

*The Astounding Tastes of My Son*  32

## IV

*The Astounding Meditations of My Son*  55

## V

*The Astounding Mind of My Son*  74

## VI

*The Astounding Beauty of My Son*  85

# LIST OF FULL-PAGE ILLUSTRATIONS

*From a Miniature*                 Frontispiece

*He reaches the island full tilt, and the cowardly island slips away from him*      3

*It is mustard and it has snapped at him and bitten him*      7

*. . . . Goes about, rollicking, in a condition the very thought of which gives me agony . . .*      13

*. . . . Lies there perfectly asleep*      17

*. . . . Suspended on the face of a precipice*      21

*. . . . A bad time for the carpet*      39

*Lay flat, and stuck his legs in the air*      49

*This astounding concentration of thought*      57

*"Thank you, darling," said my son Simon to the venerable postman*      77

*"Finking those piggyvigs in that box"*      93

# I

## *The Astounding Life of My Son*

IT is a painful thing for a father to admit, but the life led by my son is a cause of great anxiety to me. He is for ever in trouble; for ever his mother, over-indulgent, is rescuing him from some misery or disaster into which, yielding to any and every temptation, his reckless nature has plunged him.

Nor is that all; of transgressions such as these I am at least either witness or am summoned by him (he has no sense of shame) to his aid. More disturbing, I think, is the fact that he leads very largely a secret life. My son does not tell me things. I am his father and I should be his confidant; but I am not his confidant; he keeps things from me; he neither asks my advice nor listens to me when, in the kindest terms, I offer it to him.

My son ignores me.

For months now he has been living in my house, doing no work, without speaking a word to me. He never speaks to me. I do not know when he ever will speak to me.

It is all very strange and perplexing.

❧ ❧ ❧

My son Simon is seventeen months old. He has been able to walk a few weeks and it is of this period I speak when I say that the life he leads is a cause of great anxiety to me. Observing him, I have propounded to myself the very arresting thought that life for my son during his waking hours is precisely what life would be for me were I suddenly transported, defenceless, into the depths of a tropical jungle. Existence for me would be one long peril. Existence for my son is one long peril. At every step I took the terror of the unknown would be upon me. At nearly every step my son takes the unknown leaps out upon him and bangs him or throws him or bites him.

Listen and realise. My son Simon has not the faintest idea of the potentialities of *anything*. He trusts, absolutely, *everything*; and the great majority of the things with which he is surrounded reward his trust by, immediately he touches them, letting fly at him and wounding him.

[2]     As thus.

*He reaches the island full tilt, and the cowardly island slips away from him.*

He crawls excitedly under the table for something and then, having secured it, gleefully stands upright. Bang! The table has rushed down upon him and crashed his head for him.

He desires a piece of coal from the coal-box and to stoop for it he puts his hands on the fender to balance himself. Yell! The fender is hot and has jumped at him and blistered him.

He stands on tiptoe and blindly—for he cannot see the top—gropes with his fingers for anything he can reach on the breakfast table. His grope secures him something and he upsets it and its contents cover his hand. He brings down his hand well-pleased. Bright-coloured, delicious-looking stuff adorns it and he puts the whole of his hand into his mouth to enjoy it. Yell! It is mustard and it has snapped at him and bitten him.

What a life!

He essays a glorious rush across the gleaming lake of parquet to the lovely island of rug in the middle of the lake. He reaches the island, full tilt, and the cowardly island slips away from him and the parquet lake leaps up at him and thumps him *hard*, twice, once his tail and once his head.

He gets a spoon and bangs on the window ledge with it. Glorious! He puts his other hand where he is banging, and the ferocious spoon hits his other hand and wounds it. He finds that he can open a cupboard door and he has the loveliest fun in opening and shutting it. He puts his fingers around the door and shuts it like that, and the coward door catches his fingers and jams them. They get him at last, bruised and tear-stained, to his cot and he lies on his back in his cot and holds up his toy horse above his head and then lets it go; and the treacherous toy horse falls on his head and bumps it.

What a life!

Imagine an adult person enduring such a life! Imagine a life where everything you touched was liable to jump out on you and bite you! Imagine——.

I must stop. My son Simon has been playing round while I write, and he has been exploring along my bookshelves, and he has had jolly fun pulling and tugging at a volume of the Oxford Dictionary, and the savage volume has leapt out

at him and fallen on him and flattened him. And

*It is mustard and it has snapped at him and bitten him.*

his mother has dug him out and, if you please, is blaming me for it.   Why me?

What a life!

And then—resuming—there is this silence business, this distressing fact that my son will not speak to me.   In all the months that he has been staying here, doing no work, the only articulate sound that ever he has addressed directly to me is the sound "Ga-a-a!"   I know that modern children do not address their parents with the respect with which it was my love and pleasure to address mine; but I do think that "Ga-a-a!", not spoken gently but roared at me, usually thumping with a spoon or a rattle the while, is carrying equality and freedom a little far.   I know, or rather I am told, that my son *cannot* speak; but I know even more certainly that he can, and does, think, think deeply; and when I see his thoughts occupied with me (his father) I am perturbed, very much, that he should summarise them, at their termination, in "Ga-a-a!"

He thinks about me, for example, in this way. For minutes together he will sit solemnly, un-   [9]

blinkingly, staring at me; and I know perfectly well the thoughts that are in his mind. His thoughts are "Who *are* you? What place have you in this house? What do you *do* in this house? My mother waits on me hand and foot all day long. If she does not happen to be with me I have only to let fly a howl and immediately, wherever I am, she springs out of the ground and is beside me. At any hour of the night, my cot beside her bed, I have only to give the tiniest shred of a whimper and immediately she is awake and bending over me, adoring me. My nurse is my constant attendant; the maids look forward with joy to taking turns in airing me or amusing me for a bit. *You,* you do absolutely not a thing that I can see. What *are* you? What do you *do* in the house? Why do they *have* you about the place?—Ga-a-a!"

I have explained to him more than once. I have found myself rather red and guilty and mortified under this inquisition, and I have said to him, "Look here, not so much of that 'Ga-a-a' stuff, if you don't mind. What do I do? You don't understand, and I would like you, if you please, to try to understand. What do I do?

I do, in effect, *everything*.   I *keep* this house.   I work, and I earn, and with what I earn I pay for every single thing you see around you, *in*cluding your nurse and the maids *and* your mother.   Why do they have me in the house? Dash it, if it wasn't for me there wouldn't *be* any house.   Dash it, if it comes to that, if it wasn't for me there wouldn't be any *you*, not a toenail of you.   Now then?"

"Ga-a-a!"

You cannot argue with a person like that.

Another aspect of the astounding life led by my son is the astounding personal discomfort in which he is content to live.   With me neatness, tidiness, order, cleanliness, all things such as these, are carried to the point where (I sometimes think) they cease to comprise a virtue and become a vice.   My son Simon goes about, rollicking in a condition the very sight and thought of which gives me agony.   In eating an egg it is his joy apparently to plaster the whole of his face with egg, and his hate (unquestionably) to have his face relieved of the egg he has plastered. He is happy, happier, I believe, with his trousers (or whatever they call the things) half on and half off; with his vest rucked round his neck; with his essential napkin sodden and slipped to his knees; with one foot bare and a sloven sock and down-trodden shoe upon the other; with his whole person, in fact, a wreck, a tangle, an outrage and an eyesore.

What a life!

෴     ෴     ෴

There is only one moment of the day when my son Simon really unbends to me, accepts me, approves me and encourages me; and that is at night, very late, everybody else asleep, when I am going to bed and I sneak up to his cot and have a peep at him. Frequently he is awake—awake, as I like to delude myself, to see me come sneaking in; or just sufficiently between sleep and wake for me (I confess it) to whisper and touch him over the border line.

He is awake and he knows perfectly well that he ought not to be awake and that, even if he is awake, *I* ought not to be there. Tell me, if he is
[12]  not perfectly aware of this, why is it that he

*. . . . Goes about, rollicking, in a condition the very thought of which gives me agony. . . .*

conducts himself so that none shall be disturbed and wake and catch us? He lies there, I tell you, the soul and incarnation of the mischief that he knows he and I are up to together. All the normal boisterousness is hushed, all the noisy "Ga-a-a" stuff, all the wonted clambering about his cot and the hammering with his toys to attract attention. We are a couple of men together, the only men in the house, enjoying man talk and man fun such as no woman, and certainly not one of those sleeping women camped dragon-like about the house, possibly can understand; and he knows it and loves it and plays up to it. He lies there, his eyes shining, glittering, scintillating response to my every word and action; and I prod him with familiar, especial prods, and he writhes with joy; and I make exclusive, especial games for him that he and I play at this hour together, and he quivers and gloats with glee. And then, at length, he shows signs of readiness for the final crime of our criminal meeting; and I proceed to commit the final crime. He is supposed to be past the bottle stage; but a bottle and some milk are kept handy in case of midnight alarums, and I sneak the milk into the bottle, and turn his pillow, and sneak the bottle into his face, and dig the blanket in around him, and in about three minutes there he is—sound!

⌘ ⌘ ⌘

Often I watch him while he lies asleep like that. I note, with a rather dreadful movement at my heart, the perfect limbs, the perfect head, the perfect face, the perfect skin, the perfect breathing —all the sheer perfection of all that goes to make a perfect human soul that lies there perfectly asleep. With rather a dreadful movement at my heart I do discern that thus, as perfect, once lay I. My body, like my son's, once was that perfect instrument of my life; my lips, like those his lovely lips, once never had passed a hard or unkind word; my heart, my mind, like those his heart and mind of loveliest innocence, once never had held a thought base, ugly, mean. Mine once that perfect start, perfectly equipped for highest, perfect end—and now!

⌘ ⌘ ⌘

Shall I tell him? Shall I warn him? Would he listen? Would he heed?

"Ga-a-a!"

. . . . *Lies there perfectly asleep.*

## II

*The Astounding Advancement of My Son*

WHEN I last wrote of my son Simon he was seventeen months old. He is now twenty months. I wrote of him then with a touch of sharpness, a tinge of bitterness, due to certain shortcomings I had observed in him, principally the shortcoming that he ignored me and would not speak to me. I write of him now with a feeling, not so much of pride as of awe, because I now see that it has been given to me to be the father of one of the most astounding sons ever born. It is quite clear to me, and it is a very solemn and moving thought, that if he continues to advance as he has advanced in the past two months my son Simon is going to be a genius, a very pronounced and remarkable genius.

Newly interested in genius by this circumstance, I have been reading up some biographies of the great and I have observed as common to all these lives a fact which plainly shows me how remarkable a genius my son Simon is going to be. In each biography is some such phrase as "The development of his genius during those years was, etc., etc." [19]

During these *years!* Why, my son Simon develops, astoundingly, in a *day*, in an *hour*. Frequently, just while my back is turned on him, he has developed like a conjuring trick before I turn round again? I tell you, in example, that only yesterday I turned away from him while he stood in front of a high armchair with his hands on the seat, waiting to be lifted on to it. There came from him then a sound which I should describe as the agonized blending of a moan and a wail and which I know always to mean that he is up against something which *he* knows is going to end in disaster—disaster swift, sudden and calamitous.

I turned.

Believe me or believe me not, my son Simon had got one knee up on to the chair, was off the ground with the other foot, and was clawing for dear life, hung on the edge of the chair, precisely as I might claw suspended on the face of a precipice, and equally terrified.

He crashed.

Oh, yes, I grant you he crashed; he always crashes. But never mind about the crash, think of the feat! Think of that knee of his hoicked

*. . . . Suspended on the edge of a precipice.*

up on to what would be the equivalent of the Matterhorn to my knee and to where, up to that moment when I turned my back, no one imagined that he possibly could get it! What about that for rate of advancement? Tick, as you may say, goes the clock, and in that Tick that boy will have accomplished something that in the whole of his life he never has done before.

Amazing, you know, amazing!

It is, however, intellectual, not physical, development that is my theme when I speak of the astounding advancement of my son. Personally I have no higher wish or ambition for him than that he should hit one into the pavilion at Lord's or drop a goal against Scotland at Twickenham (what ambition *could* be higher?); but I realise that more serious achievements than these are necessary to the advancement of the world; and that my son Simon is going to advance the world at a rate calculated to make it (the world) pretty well dizzy no one watching him in these past two months possibly could doubt.

I tell you, in example, that after months of dumbness my son Simon is now pouring out articulate words at a rate and with a precision that

I cannot believe has ever before been equalled.
Up to a few weeks ago he was what I may call a
Three Word Man.

Mum-mum-mum,
Da-da-da and
Ga-a-a!

were his three words and I was beginning to have
the gloomy apprehension that he was going to be
a Three Word Man all his life.

How wrong I was! I tell you that quite
suddenly, biding his own time and choosing it
with considered deliberation (What character!)
he began letting fly words with what I can only
describe as the sweep and range of a sheer master
of the English language. And what a brain he
then revealed! Quite clearly he has been storing
up in that brain all the words he has constantly
been hearing and now, at his own will and pleasure, he is releasing them.

How many words he had thus stored his mother
and I only began to realise on the terrific and
astounding occasion on which, quite suddenly
and quite clearly, he produced the word "There!"
Recovered from our amazement and from our awe
at owning such a child, we used his astounding

knowledge of the word as a species of divining-rod into the unknown depths of his intellect.

"Where is your nose, Simon?"

Believe me or believe me not, that amazing child clapped the flat of his hand to his nose and cried "There!"

I mean to say, What a brain!

"Where are your eyes?   Where are your shoes? Where is the bread?   Where is the butter? Where the door?   Where the window?"

Believe me or believe me not, every time the correct indication and every time "There!"

I mean to say, *Talk* about genius!

You know, I was so overcome at the genius thus shown, so saturated with awe at being the father of such a son, that I went straight upstairs to my Dictionary of National Biography to look out the place in it which my son Simon at this rate is bound to occupy.   They will fit him, I find, as that monument of the great is at present edited, into Volume X and between HUTCHIN-SON, ROGER (d. 1555), and HUTCHINSON, THOMAS (1689–1769).

Pretty wonderful, you know!

Pretty wonderful—and all else I have to say

about it at the moment is that how long Hutchinson, Roger, and Hutchinson, Thomas, have stood in their present juxtaposition in the D.N.B. I do not know and to tell you the honest truth I do not greatly care.  My sole concern with them is to warn them that when HUTCHINSON, SIMON, comes along they will be separated for ever by, I should say, at least a dozen pages.

And you know the very odd thing in this connection is that his mother and I always knew, from the very first, that he was going to be famous. Something seemed to tell us that he was and that was why we named him Simon, and only Simon, no other name.  His father, you see, had dragged three initials through life (and look at him now!) so we decided that his son should have but one and, in actual practice, not even one, because when a man has but a single Christian name it is pretty certain that he will always get the whole of it, not the initial; and of all single names Simon seemed to us the most impressive for a man as remarkable as our son unquestionably was going to be and, as each day proves, unquestionably *is*.  We imagined it—SIMON HUTCHINSON—on a plate in Harley Street, and over chambers in Lincoln's

Inn, and in the list (Barons) of Birthday Honours, and on a plaque over the house he was born in, and on a tablet in Westminster Abbey, and in all sorts of places among the seats of the mighty, and it seemed to us, wherever we imagined it, well, *right*. Well, I mean to say, just have a look at it for yourself in one or two aspects and see how absolutely right it is:

Simon Hutchinson, not out . . . 100.
Simon Hutchinson, K.C.
Simon Hutchinson, M.D.
Simon Hutchinson, R.A.
Sir Simon Hutchinson.
Admiral Sir Simon Hutchinson.
General Sir Simon Hutchinson.
Simon, Lord Hutchinson.

Pretty good, eh?

Precisely what profession he will illuminate we do not yet know. It may be music. Indications are before us that it may be as a great composer that he will burst upon the world. He will sit perfectly still listening to music, perfectly still, not even an eyelid blinking. From the moment when at a quite hideous hour of the morning he starts upright in his cot, wider awake than his father is at midday, from then until, wider awake than ever, he stands upright in his cot, refusing to go to sleep in the evening, he is, with intervals of exhausted slumber, *never* still. He is *always* moving. If he is roped into his chair or his pram and cannot move his legs he moves his arms, wildly. If he is so constrained that he can move neither arms nor legs he moves, he convulses, his whole body. It is like having an earthquake in your arms, and about as easy to hold. But when music is made! When we turn on the wireless or when his mother plays the piano my son Simon will sit on my knee, still as a mouse, hushed as a church, and in his eyes a depth of wonder, deep as magic pools.

So perhaps it is music.

Or perhaps it is books. He adores a picture book. He squeals with delight when I produce his books. If you could hear him snort through his nose when the picture shows a pig, or produce astounding gobbling noises when it shows a turkey, you would know as I know that he is reading, voraciously, and thrilled to the bone. So perhaps it is books; perhaps he is going to be [28] what a woman of our village once told some one

of me—that I was "only a literature gentleman."
Or perhaps—but what is the good of guessing?
The final thing to establish is that, whatever he is
destined for, he must, at his present rate, adorn;
the final thing to be told is that, in these few weeks
of this astounding advancement of his, he has
shown me—my son Simon—three mysteries
which but for him I should have gone through life,
yes, and to the other side of death, and never seen.

Three mysteries—first, singing birds released
from lovely cages into lovely flight and song;
next, glimpse of Heaven; next, those baby
angels who, as I believe, throng in their little
nightgowns on the wide steps of Heaven to greet
and lead within the old and very tired folk who
come to enter.

The singing birds: I have described how, in
these days, my son Simon is for ever, suddenly and
unexpectedly, producing some new word.  It is
when I sit and think of him opening that quite
exquisite mouth of his, and in that quite exquisite
pipe of his emitting some new sound, that I have
a vision as of the opening of a lovely cage and
the winging out of lovely singing birds such as
my world, as least, never before has seen or heard.  [29]

The glimpse of Heaven: I have spoken of how he will sit, perfectly still, profoundly absorbed, listening to music. It is when so he sits, thus motionless, thus occupied, upon my knee, my arm about him, my eyes upon those deep-with-wonder eyes of his, only the two of us in all the world, one stained, one spotless, perfect, pure, that I am made aware within myself that I am then as near to Heaven as ever mortal of my sort may hope to be.

Those baby angels: These he gives me when I hear him awake shortly after he has been put away in his cot for the night and is supposed to be asleep. I open the door of his room and stand there saying no word, fixing him with a stern, reproving eye. He is standing upright, his tiny, lovely hands upon the cot rail, his snowy nightgown just above his small and lovely toes. He knows that I am stern; he knows I am reproving him; he knows (for he has had it), that I may growl out stern and shocked reproach.

So do you know what he does?

He makes his lovely face more lovely with the loveliest smile that ever eyes and lips joined mirth

to make, and he chatters, chatters, chatters,

endless, wordless explanations of his wakefulness until (unable to hold out the more) I smile response and go to him and know that I am holding out my hands to hands held out to me as by those baby angels in their little nightgowns, thronging the wide steps of Heaven, to those whom they stand there to welcome.

My son Simon!

## III

### *The Astounding Tastes of My Son*

 CANNOT say of my son Simon that he is now (two years and two months) developing likes and dislikes, tastes and predilections, estimations and opinions, because from the very first nothing in all the astonishing mystery and marvel of him has astounded me so much as the clarity and assurance of his views on life and of his tastes and opinions in regard to all that he sees about him in general. It has taken me years and years to make up my mind on certain subjects and even now I frequently change it, deciding that I have been wrong. Not so my son Simon. From the very beginning my son Simon knew what he liked and what he disliked, and said so. He arrived with his mind made up, and said so. The very first breath he drew, the absolute first, number one, original breath was, if you will believe me, used for expression of his opinion on a matter about which I, with nearly fifty years to my discredit, am still uncertain: his opinion, I mean, on life spelt with a capital L—Life.

[32]    I was out in the garden at the time (9.20 p.m.

of a winter's night) suffering, because I was the man, the mental share of that crisis of our union whose physical anguish, because she was the woman, was being endured by the creature more dear to me than all creation, when high above the lamentable sounds which had driven me from the house and which came to me now through the slightly opened bedroom window that I watched—high above these came suddenly a voice, a roar, a defiant bellow, an outraged yell of hate, indignation, fury and disgust. It was a voice that never before had spoken. It was the voice of my son Simon arriving in the world and saying what he thought about the world. It was a voice that never before had spoken but that spoke now with the conviction of one steeped in wisdom and in experience of life and announcing uncompromisingly, abusively, violently what he thought of life—namely that life was a burden and an outrage, a trap and a snare, a delusion, an imposition, a torment and a nuisance, a thing altogether damnable, insufferable, intolerable and not to be endured.

Knew all that, said all that—and only about two and a half seconds old, mind you!

Yes, my son Simon arrived, as I have shown, with his mind made up and he has persisted from thence onwards in the same flat and uncompromising resolution of opinion (good or bad) on all with which or with whom he has come in contact. From the very first it never was the least use to tell my son Simon what he ought to think about a thing. He knew. I should say there can be no words more familiar to him at his present age than the words "Isn't it lovely?" As he advanced, and as at the present period of his life still he advances, through changes of diet, of dress, of discipline, of deportment, always, as each change is introduced to him, it is introduced with the ingratiating inquiry. "Isn't it lovely?"; and before he reached ability to reply in articulate words I should say there was no sound more familiar to those who have the rearing of him than, if unable to agree, the roar with which he would express "No, it is not lovely. It is loathsome. It is abominable. Get me out of the infernal thing. Take the foul thing away from me. If you think it so jolly nice wear it yourself, eat it yourself, do it yourself. I loathe it. I hate the sight of it. Take it away!"

A pretty useful roar, you know, to convey all that in one blast and he still uses it sometimes; but he now can string words together in expression of his likes and dislikes; and two of his very earliest sentences, suddenly and astoundingly produced, were in expression of his views on the sacred subject of his father. He knows already, I have here to say, that a sharp diversity of opinion exists between his father and himself on certain matters, notably on those of noise, of spilling things, of smashing things, of hurling things, of fidgeting and of wriggling. All these my son Simon revels in; all these his father (a splendid but a temperamental fellow) abominates; and conflict of view between the twain is often sharp. His father, in such conflict, has the advantage of him in that he can say, and if necessary enforce, what he thinks. He has the advantage of his father in that he does not care fourpence what his father thinks; and what, for his own part, he thinks about his father was revealed the other day when, suddenly gifted with speech during an argument between us relative to hurling a wastepaper basket across the room, he announced it.

Abandoning the argument, he turned from it [35]

and from his father and, red-faced and injured-browed, stalked solemnly across to his mother.

"Don't like Daddy!" he announced.

This was his opinion as to his father divulged to a third person. Later in the same day, still, no doubt, brooding upon it, he stated to me his taste on the same matter as man to man, straight to my face. There is a fixed moment after tea at which I go up to my study to play at my work until dinner and my son Simon goes into the drawing-room to work at his play with his mother until his bedtime. On my way on this occasion thus to give rein to my genius I looked in at the drawing-room door, hoping to be invited either by my wife or my son not to overstrain myself but to rest my genius for a while in gentle dalliance in their company.

I looked in.

My son Simon had collected every cushion in the room into a repulsively untidy heap on the floor and with them a dozen or so other articles of use or beauty which should not have been scattered about among the cushions and were in no way improved by being scattered among the cushions. I had entered the room with, in my face, that kind, gentle look which so endears me to my friends, but the sight of that repulsive confusion on the floor banished the look and replaced it by a look which my son Simon did not misinterpret, did not like, and proceeded therefore to deal with in an uncompromising way with which he deals with all his tastes. He looked up at me from his hideous mess. Disgust met disgust.

"Daddy go upstairs," he said.

Upstairs or downstairs, in his nursery or in our dining room, with similar uncompromising directness, my son Simon expresses his taste in the matter of food. If he is in mood to eat he will eat. If he is not in mood to eat no task is so absurd a waste of time as to try to coax him to eat. A dish is set before him, a spoonful from the dish is carried to his mouth; he firmly shuts his mouth and refuses to receive it. His mother pretends to eat of the spoonful. "Oh, isn't it lovely!" declares his mother. His father pretends to eat of it. "Oh, isn't it lovely!" exclaims his father. The spoon is conveyed to his horse, to his cow, to his gollywog, to each and all of the toys which may be attending his meal with him; and [37]

ventriloquially "Oh, isn't it lovely!" horse, cow
and gollywog declare.

My son Simon, relaxing his jaws, watches this
procession of the spoon with enormous interest
and pleasure, smiles to see his mother's pleasure in
the spoonful, smiles to see his father's pleasure,
smiles radiantly to witness the pleasure in the
spoonful of his horse, his cow, his gollywog and
every thing that is his—and swiftly and dexter-
ously the spoon is plunged from the last of his
toys straight into the middle of the radiant smile.

Too late!

It is his clenched teeth that the spoon
encounters. His smile has gone. His brow is
dark. His face is ominously red. "Take it
away!" commands my son Simon; and convert-
ing himself into a spineless, India-rubber freak,
shoots down in his chair and would shoot out of
it but for the bar that checks him, the grabbing
hands that clutch him as he checks.

"Oh, but isn't it lovely!"

"Take it avay!  Take it avay!"

Tea, I am happy to say, is the only meal eaten
by me in the company of my son Simon; and
I am happy to say it because meals at my time of

. . . . *A bad time for the carpet.*

life are solemn affairs to be enjoyed with long-accustomed ritual and decorum; whereas at my son Simon's time of life they appear to me to be no more than a continuation of his normal round of play enlivened (for him) by the thrusting at him of spoonfuls of food whenever he can be caught and steadied for the process.   He starts a meal sitting in a chair, takes it thus for perhaps as long as three minutes, and continues it then while trotting round the table by having it stabbed at him in the manner and in the circumstances aforesaid.   What happens to it if and when it has been successfully stabbed home and has not missed his mouth and shot past cheek and ear on to the floor is a matter of entire uncertainty. My son Simon may swallow it; he may carry it about in his mouth as complacently as if his mouth were a pocket and the spoonful a penny; or he may, having accepted it on the run and in one stride of the run, at the next stride incontinently and unconcernedly flip it out with his tongue, indifferent as to upon what or upon whom it may fall.   I know nothing about his other meals, but of his tea I would say that it is a good time for the dog, a bad time for the carpet, and for my   [41] son Simon himself a time devoted to everything and anything except the assimilation of food.

I do not, mind you, blame him. I blame, need I say, the women with whom he is surrounded. They are not firm. They give way to him. A child is born into this world without knowledge of either right or wrong and it is, or it may be made, just as natural for him (I maintain) to do things in the right, wholesome and proper way as to do them in the way wrong, unwholesome and improper. I get little chance of demonstrating my views but I had one recently, and in public, which was, up to a point, a triumphant vindication of my theories and which only showed (up to that point) towards what dangers the country is rushing by passing governance more and more out of the hands of men and more and more into the hands of women.

Some relatives, on the occasion of this great demonstration, came to lunch and as their number included one of years not many more than my son Simon's, and as my brother (his uncle) basely threw in his suffrage with the women's party, it was voted with a single dissentient (myself) that my son Simon also should attend the meal. All went—the admission was presently dragged from me—quite reasonably well. My son Simon, awed by the strange faces amidst which he found himself, quelled by the gloomy eye with which I regarded him across the joint, handed out a surprising exhibition of stillness in his chair, quietude of his usually mischievous and marauding hands, rigidity of his normally banging and drumming legs. He was exhibited, enthusiastically, by his mother, cautiously, as time went on, by his father, as a model child; and so long as his part remained that of watching the company feed itself model he continued to be.

The moment arrived when himself was to be fed and immediately he was no longer model.

A delicious dish was set before him and in the prescribed formula ("Oh, isn't it lovely!") he was informed by every tongue at the table how delicious it was. No use. His mind was made up. It was not lovely. Five to one in numbers and about one hundred and seventy to two in years were against him on the point, but he was equal to the five, equal to the one seventy. Two spoonfuls of the delicious dish he accepted; [43]

then the rigid jaws, the reddened face, the darkened brow, the spineless and India-rubber shoots into the depths of his chair and below them.

Round to each member of the company, including his hobbyhorse, goes his devoted mother with the spoon:

His Uncle: "Isn't it lovely!"
" Aunt:      "   "   "
" Cousin:   "   "   "
" Father:   "   "   "
" Mother:   "   "   "
" Horse:    "   "   "

She completes the circle. Entranced, my son Simon has sat observing her; and swiftly and strongly plunges she the spoon into the smile with which he has watched this delightfully extended journey of the spoon. Too late! More swiftly and more strongly closes the ivory portcullis which defends the gateway to the erstwhile smiling mouth. Defeat! Humiliation!

Then arises my son Simon's father, superb in majestic mastery and calm. "Give me the spoon. Let me do it. All this fooling about is simply pandering to him, ruining him. What he wants, all he wants, is firmness—kind firmness, firm kindness. Leave him to me."

Awed, they leave him to me.

"Simon," I inform him, my voice calm but deep, stern but kind, "Simon, this is very nice. Dad says this is very nice and therefore it is very nice. Dad will give it to Simon and Simon will eat it."

My son Simon looks at me. I !ook at my son Simon. It is an awful moment. The battle of our wills is joined. Our whole future relations depend upon the issue. It is an awful moment; but it is more awful for my son Simon than it is for me. Not much more awful but just a shade more awful and that shade sufficient. He cannot maintain the power of my eye. My will is triumphant. He opens his mouth like a lamb. I plunge home the loaded spoon. The whole company watch us, dumbfounded, awed. I withdraw the spoon, empty. A gasp of wonder arises from the company. My wife's gasp is the loudest gasp and I am glad that it is the loudest gasp. I have proved my principle.

It is for me unquestionably a great, a supreme moment, but I conduct myself with gentle grace,

with modest charm; I neither vaunt myself nor am I puffed up. Paying no heed whatsoever to the murmured tributes of awe, of wonder, of congratulation, confining myself solely to my son, "Good boy!" I say to my son. "Very good boy! Dad said it was lovely and Simon sees how lovely it is because Dad said it was. More!"

Another loaded spoon drives home, emerges empty; another, another. Four loaded spoons.

It is indeed a great, an apotheosistical moment for me. I am only an author and the company thinks of me (I know) as only an author and not much of a one at that. But, superficial, too close to me to judge me at my true worth, it sees in me now qualities with which it has never credited me—strong, silent, he-man qualities, and its tribute to them is written on every one of its faces.

I am not, as I have said, puffed up by their tributes; but, as impressively I charge my fifth spoonful, I feel that I am entitled to, and I cannot forbear, a few sober, telling words. "You see," I address them, "what it is. The boy requires only a firm hand, a kind, firm hand, and he will do anything he is told. He loves me but, because

I am firm, he also respects me and obeys me. He is not afraid of me, but he realizes that he owes a duty to me, and at my desire he pays me that duty. He——"

*Flick!*

Something flies from the mouth of my son Simon and explodes itself like a burst egg on the table before him. It is my four spoonfuls of delicious food. My son Simon has not swallowed them. He has accumulated them in his mouth. He has formed them with his tongue into what in medical phraseology is termed a bolus and he has braced his tongue behind the bolus and—*flick!*—projected the bolus with negligent, contemptuous, disdainful jerk on to the tablecloth before him. . . .

It is of my son Simon, not of myself, that I am writing, so I will pass over with the contempt it merits the howl of ribald laughter at my expense with which 'this painful, not to say disgusting, exhibition was greeted by the company assembled at my board; and I will emphasize instead that what at once stung me most and caused me most to realize the astounding character of my son Simon was the (to repeat myself) negligent, con- [47]

temptuous, disdainful air with which the flick of the disgusting bolus was performed. My son Simon neither quailed at what he had done nor exulted in what he had done—he just did it and abided by it. He just flipped out the bolus of food as you might toss aside a book, or a penny into a beggar's hat, or a cherrystone from between your fingers—just that, and then waited calm, dispassionate, unmoved, slightly bored, entirely uninterested, for the fifth spoonful.

There was no fifth spoonful. My son Simon had announced his taste in the matter of food fed to him by his father, and there was, in so far as his father was concerned, nothing to be done but to accept his indication of his taste.

What other, indeed, can you do with tastes and opinions so pronounced as those of my son Simon but accept them? Take, finally, his tastes on the much larger matter of his future career. They are entirely different from any that we had hoped to discover and encourage in him, but so assured they are that we feel we have no option but to concur in them. It took me till I was more than twenty to decide definitely what [48] should be my walk in life; and to this day I have

*Lay flat, and stuck his legs in the air.*

only to read the views of professional critics on my books to be informed that, despite rather more than two decades given to choice of what I was best suited for, I obviously chose wrong. In slightly more than two years only my son Simon, on the other hand, has chosen deliberately and purposefully. He is going to be a ——

One moment. While I am on the matter I will illustrate, if I may, on another point the astounding development in my son Simon of tastes which it took me to manhood and more to cultivate. I was as much as about thirty before there seized me the taste for doing physical exercises as a daily morning practice. My son Simon, watching me at them, was seized of the taste when but a shade over two. One of my exercises is the familiar one called "press-ups"— extending the body between the hands and toes and lowering and raising on the arms, lifting each leg alternately at the same time. Another is lying full length on the back, then raising the legs and touching the floor behind the head with the toes.

My son Simon, watching me at these with the enormous interest with which he watches all I do when we are alone together, now, if you please, himself does them. We were at tea the other day, his mother and I, Simon playing around and receiving stabs of food as described above, when "What *is* he doing?" his mother suddenly exclaimed. He was doing press-ups. He had the top of his head on the floor between his hands, his small stern pointed at the ceiling, and in this position with enormous gravity was kicking out first one leg then the other behind him; then lay flat and stuck his legs in the air and lowered and raised them; then arose and continued the play he had interrupted in order to perform these evolutions. Now, at any moment of the day, and engaged in whatsoever occupation, he suddenly will break off, do his exercises, and resume what had previously been engaging him.

Two years and two months old!

Is it a Samson that he is going to be?

No, he is not going to be a Samson; he is going to be a groom.

My son Simon is crazy about horses. He thinks of nothing but horses; he plays at nothing but horses; he appears to dream of nothing but horses. All day long he is astride of something—

anything, from a footstool to the arm of the chair, from his mother's head while she lies asleep when he has crawled into her bed in the morning to his father's feet while his father reclines in a chair apparently asleep but really thinking out a masterpiece of literature—astride of anything he can get his legs across, gripping with his knees in the most approved fashion, clicking with his tongue till you would think his tongue must be sore. At night he will awake and lie there in the dark, perfectly content, utterly happy, "Tchk, tchk; tchk, tchk!" until he falls asleep again. When he is out in his push-cart he has only a profoundly solemn stare for everything (except one thing) that presents itself to his gaze. A more estimating, debating, totally unmoved stare than he gives to the common objects of his outings —including even, when he meets them, his parents —could not be seen, I am convinced, on the face of the Lord Chief Justice listening to counsel.

But let a horse appear! Let a horse even be heard! "Gee-gee!" shouts my son Simon, face ablaze, head nearly screwed off in the horse's direction, arms gripping the sides of his coach, legs convulsing his body to obtain him a better view.

"Gee-gee! Gee-gee!" and abandons himself to sheer ecstasy of delight.

So, yes, he is going to be a groom—a groom, not a rider to hounds, a polo player, or any other type of gentleman rider, for no one but a groom or a butcher boy clicks his tongue, "Tchk, tchk!" when in the saddle, and the "Tchk, tchk!" is more than half the fun of the exercise to my son Simon, so groom and not gentleman rider it obviously is to be. Yes, a groom! All our fond and ambitious plans for him are as nought. We are withdrawing his name from the great public school for which we had put it down; we are spending on ourselves the hard-earned money we had started to save for the expensive education which devotedly we had intended for him; and we are doing instead what little we can think of to help him towards the career of his choice and his aptitude. It is not much that we can do but such as it is it is self-sacrificial and has given us a pang. We are abandoning his dignified and inspiring name of Simon. We are trying to teach ourselves to call him by the good groom's name that will be useful to him when he applies for his first job.

[54]  My son—Sam.

## IV

### *The Astounding Meditations of My Son*

IN a childhood book of mine was a picture of Sir Isaac Newton gazing at a fallen apple and meditating, so the legend with the picture said, the thoughts that led him therefrom to his discovery of the force of gravity. It must have made a considerable impression on me because it is good forty and five years since I had that book and yet, brought back to me by astounding manifestations in my son Simon, I can see the picture now as clearly as I saw it then—Sir Isaac Newton in a bright red cloak, sitting in a bright green orchard, gazing fixedly upon a bright yellow apple which has plunged from a bright brown tree on to the bright green grass with which the orchard is carpeted.

Impressive thought! There in my mental eye he has sat all these years, my mental eye shut upon him, and suddenly comes along my son Simon with traits that fill me with a great awe and wonder; and, wondering, I turn my physical eye away from my son exhibiting these traits and my mental eye flies open and there the great Sir Isaac is—watching [55] his bright yellow apple in his bright red cloak and bidding me, as it were, to watch my son Simon saying to me, as it were, "Mark that boy of yours. He is one of us."

I believe he is!

Saying to me, as it were, "Note the resemblance between him and me."

I do note the resemblance. It is most striking. It thrills me.

I do not, mind you, pretend, nor, when my son Simon is hailed as one of history's greatest savants, and journalists come down to interview his poor old father, will I ever (I hope) pretend that I have ever seen my son Simon wearing a bright red cloak and gazing at a bright yellow apple fallen in a bright green field; but I have seen him time and again recently plunged into meditations at a depth from which nothing but his own inclinations will rescue him, and I have heard him pronounce, if not the result, at least the subject of those meditations with a solemnity of voice and a profundity of air which, when I realize that he is only not-quite-two-and-a-half, cause me positively to tremble at thought of what he will be coming out with when he is the

*This astounding concentration of thought.*

age at which Sir Isaac Newton came out with the principles of the force of gravity.

It began, this astounding concentration of thought on some particular phenomenon, back in that very cold spell which you and your plumber may remember sealed all the water taps last February. My son Simon, taken out on one of those perishing, iron-bound, knife-edged days, was taken as usual past a horse trough which, with his passion for horses, long had been an object of deepest interest to him, and which, with his limitation of vocabulary, has always been referred to by him as "Gee-gees' water."

Well, on this particular day he found this trough frozen. He was informed by his nurse that the substance he now saw in the trough and was permitted to touch and stand upon was called ice; and, lifted back into his perambulator, he lapsed at once (his nurse testifies) into a species of trance, hypnosis, stupor or coma from which nothing during the remainder of the outing could by any means arouse him.

In this shape he was brought home. He was hurried home. His nurse thought he was ill.

[59]

He was not ill. He was—well, mark closely, please, what follows, and see for yourself what was up with him.

It is his mother's habit on his return from his daily airing to bound out to him from wheresoever she may be, to enfold him in her arms in his pram, to lift him on high and to her bosom, to embrace him, and, fondling him, to inquire of him where he has been and what he has seen. All this she went through as usual on the day in question; and she noticed (she affirms) the remarkable change in him as she did so. Normally responding always with smiles, with crows, with chuckles, hugs, and eager though disjointed descriptive matter relative to her questions, he presented now an air, a countenance and a silence of profoundest abstraction and introspection. Having eyes he appeared to see not, ears to hear not, lips and certainly spake not. What was the matter with him?

Suddenly he declared it.

Speaking with a slow and portentous utterance, impossible of adequate description but rather as one chiding his mother for troubling him with such triflings and such vanities when such enormous things were toward, he delivered himself of the following stupendous statement.

"Ice on the gee-gees' water."

You see what it was. Newton saw that apple fall and sat deep in the meditation in which my childhood picture presents him; my son Simon saw that water frozen and plunged forthwith into that stupor of speculation in which I am trying to show him.

And only not-quite-two-and-a-half, mind you! Listen further.

It is the custom of his father, never one to commit the folly of overwork, to appear at about this time from his study, to join the group gathered about the perambulator, to prod his son with ticklish fingers, to lift him on high and tell him how huge he is growing, to set him down and then also to inquire of him in what manner he has been amusing himself and wherewithal he has been passing his time. His father, scrupulously avoiding over-strain, appears, prods, lifts, set down, inquires. Solemnly, reprovingly is gazed upon by his son. Portentously, staggeringly is informed by his son.

"Ice on the gee-gees' water."

His father, I tell you, reeled.

I tell you that the appearance of that ice on that water of those gee-gees changed the whole life and disposition of my son Simon. For weeks he appeared to think of nothing else. Whenever spoken to and on whatever subject, listening with apparent attention, almost invariably his reply would show that he had not been listening at all, that his mind had been entirely occupied with the phenomenon which, like the fallen apple to Newton, precipitated him into the depths of mysterious speculations never before explored by the human mind—to all, to anything and to everybody, "Ice on the gee-gees' water," he would respond.

The effect on his interlocutor sometimes was devastating. I can give, in instance, the effect upon myself when the astounding asseveration was dropped crushingly upon me at the termination of an entertainment which I had then but recently organised for my son and which, up to then, had been received by my son with high approval; the entertainment of story-telling.

[62] You will imagine that, with story-writing as my

profession, the invention of stories for such as my son Simon would be as easy to me as clipping my finger nails; but you would imagine wrong. Story-writing is always a pain and a labour to me. I will squirm for three hours together in closest concentration over a novel and produce, frequently, no more than a single page of manuscript in all that time; but my worst trials in that respect I found to be as nothing compared with the brainwork necessitated for my first stories told to my son. I was, you see, almost hopelessly limited, not only in range of subjects within the comprehension of my listener, but in range of words. My son Simon, when I told him my first story, knew about fourteen nouns and three verbs. I give myself (I think) no airs in the matter of comparison between myself and my fellow novelists over stories for the narration of which we have the entire Oxford Dictionary at our equal disposal; but I will bet money that no author, contemporary, dead or to come, will do much better than me in fourteen nouns and three verbs only.

I will give you the story, if I may, as I now, my son's vocabulary slightly extended, tell it; and  [ 63 ]

you must imagine my son sitting in raptest attention, eyes starting from his head, brow knotted in
concentration, tiny hands clutching tiny, naked
knees, listening to me; and imagine him also
breaking in, thrilled to the marrow, at points at
which he has learnt to break in and for which he
eagerly waits.

"Once there was a boy" (I declare) "called
Neddy. He had a mum and he had a dad.
One day Neddy had tea with his mum and dad.
They had bread and butter, and milk, and toast
and cake with sugar on it. Neddy had some.
And while Neddy was having some Neddy said,
'Please, I want some jam.' But his mum said,
'No, Neddy, you cannot have jam because when
you had jam it made you——' "

"Sick!" shouts my son Simon, who has been
through it himself and has high relish apparently
in the thought of Neddy also suffering.

"Yes, sick," I affirm. "So then Neddy said,
'Please, I want some honey.' So his dad said,
'No, Neddy, you cannot have honey because last
time you had honey it made you——' "

"Sick!" bawls my son Simon, and I straighten
[64]   him from the perilous position into which the

ecstasy of the moment has thrown him, and continue.

"Yes, sick. So after tea what did Neddy do?"

"Down de tairs!" shouts my son Simon, thrilled to the bone with expectation, and, with voice deepened to the proper horror of the deed, I agree to this.

"Yes, he went down the stairs to the door where his mum kept the jam, and he opened the door and on the shelf was a pot of jam and he took the pot of jam and he had no spoon so what did he do?"

"Put hand in de jam!"

"Yes, Naughty Neddy," say I, giving Master Edward now the title which is also the title of the story ("Naughty Neddy"). "Yes, Naughty Neddy put his hand in the jam, ate the jam with his hand, and was horrible with jam on his face and on his clothes, and all of a sudden he ——"

"Dopped de jam!" bawls my son Simon, crimson, and has to be straightened again.

"Yes, dropped the jam crash and bang; and his dad heard it and his dad——" Edward's father, I must here pause to remark, has points of [65]

irritability and impulsiveness similar to my own—
"and his dad roared out 'Neddy! What you
doing?' and what did Naughty Neddy say?"

"Please, Dad," shouts my son Simon in tone
of highest glee such as certainly the unhappy
Edward never would have used, "Please, Dad, I
dopped de jam!"

"Yes," I return, my voice charged to suffoca-
tion with Edward's tears. "Yes—'Please, Dad,
I've dropped the jam!' 'Dropped the jam!'
roared Naughty Neddy's dad. 'You naughty
Neddy! I'll give you walloping whacks!' and
down the stairs came his dad, rushing and
crashing, and caught hold of Naughty Neddy
and gave him walloping whacks, and Naughty
Neddy howled and bawled and roared and
jumped and bumped."

And "Wasn't that a nice story?" I always
end; and "Volloping vacks! Volloping
vacks!" shouted with ecstatic delight and with
Mr. Weller's principle of spelling it "vith a wee",
is the tribute always paid by my son Simon to
show how nice it was.

Well, by this and by that and for one reason
and another, the story of Naughty Neddy was

not told to my son Simon for over a fortnight after his first pondering of the phenomenon of ice on the gee-gees' water. I was away for a bit, for one thing, and I came back with a new picture book for another; but the afternoon arrived when Naughty Neddy repeated his shocking behaviour again; and as my son Simon's vocabulary increases daily, giving me greater scope for my art, I was able to elaborate it in its early stages with a minuteness of detail and a warmth of colour such as it never before had had, and was rewarded with a depth of attention from my son Simon such as I never before had received. He sat wide-eyed, unblinking, drinking it in with a rapture far outdoing that on the face of the central figure in the well-known painting "The Boyhood of Raleigh," too deeply absorbed (with an author's excusable pride I noticed) even to fill in the usual pauses with his usual shouts. Flattered, triumphant, I came to my stirring end —"And down the stairs came his dad, rushing and crashing, and caught hold of Naughty Neddy and gave him walloping whacks and Naughty Neddy howled and roared and bawled and jumped and bumped."

"There! Wasn't that a nice story?" I cried.

"Ice on the gee-gees' water," pronounced my son Simon.

All through my impassioned story, all through Naughty Neddy's trials and tribulations, my son Simon, as Newton beside that apple tree, had been sitting beside that trough!

And only not-quite-two-and-a-half, mind you!

Writing away from books of reference, I am unable to know what age Sir Isaac Newton was when he sat in that bright red cloak in that bright green orchard and meditated upon that bright yellow apple fallen from that bright brown tree; but that he was very considerably more than not-quite-two-and-a-half I am quite certain; and if it was by pure concentration of thought upon that apple that he arrived at the principles of the force of gravity, what my son Simon, concentrating as he did upon that ice on those gee-gees' water at the age of little more than two, will arrive at when he is Newton's age in the picture, passes all human speculation and fills me with a very great awe indeed. Whether it is going to be some hitherto unsuspected phenomenon connected with [68] freezing point that he is to discover, or whether his concentration on that is merely, as it were, practice for concentration on some other matter, I cannot, of course, say. I know on the one hand that millions of people have seen ice on the gee-gees' water and made out of it nothing more than appears to the eye; but I know on the other that millions of people saw millions of apples fall from millions of trees without discovering what Isaac Newton discovered; and it is to me a profoundly moving thought that childhood books of the future may show my son Simon swaddled in a camel's-hair rug in a dark blue pram gazing at a frozen horse trough with beneath the picture the inscription

*"Simon Hutchinson meditating the principles of (?) when first observing ice on the gee-gees' water."*

*Or*, as I have said, his absorption for weeks and weeks on that ice on those gee-gees' water may have been the first expression of a profundity of thought which ultimately will wrench an epoch-making discovery out of some other matter; and to this view I am rather inclined because about a month ago a second phenomenon presented itself to my son Simon's observation and has ridden him ever since precisely as did the first.  [69]

He is very fond of cows and, his early life being passed in a dairy-farming part of the country, is well accustomed to cows and in no degree afraid of them.  It happened about two months after the ice on the gee-gees' water affair that he was being motored from the place of dairy farms to a place by the sea, and that the car, in the course of the journey, was held up by a drove of bullocks which surrounded the car and, with mien very different from the amiable cows to which he is accustomed, thrust their heads, horns, quarters and tails all about the windows of the car, causing my son Simon to exhibit signs of unrest, discomfort and alarm.

He was told that they were bullocks.

The car ran on about thirty miles before he spoke.  A halt was then made for lunch, food was set before him and with a strange and unusual solemnity and silence he partook of it.  His meals (as I have presented in a previous article) are normally a severe trial of everybody's patience but his own; on this occasion he accepted mutely, automatically, immovably every spoonful that was introduced to him.  He received, masticated, swallowed as if he did not know that he was receiving, masticating, swallowing. It was like putting food into a machine. He displayed no interest in it whatsoever, nor in anything that was said to him or that was going on about him. Something appeared to be on his mind.

Something was on his mind, a mind that might have been Newton's occupied with the apple, and presently he disclosed it.

"Don't like those bullocks on the road," he said.

His first words since, an hour and a half before, the bullocks had been observed; his last words until, nearly three hours later, the journey was ended: "Don't like those bullocks on the road!"

His new habitation was reached. He was shown his new rooms, carried around to be made acquainted with all the appointments of his new rooms, held up to be shown the superb spectacle of the ocean to be seen from the windows of his new rooms.

"There, Simon! Look at that. That is called the sea. Water like in Simon's bath, lots and lots and lots of water like in Simon's bath, called the sea; and to-morrow Simon will go down there and take off his shoes and stockings and walk in the sea, called paddling in the sea. Say 'sea,' Simon. Say 'Paddle in the sea.'"

"Don't like those bullocks on the road," said Simon.

It was his new absorption, his new apple, his new phenomenon in which, evidently, were revealed to him signs and portents never previously revealed to the human mind. He was amidst scenes, surroundings, entertainments, species, as entirely new to him as would be to me all that I would perceive about me on a visit to Mars or if I slept to awake in the world as it will be a hundred years hence. He clung amidst them all to the phenomenon of bullocks on the road and to his disapproval of bullocks on the road. He had been full fortnight at the seaside when the day fell perfect for the treat long promised him and in every thrilling detail described to him—a row in a boat.

He was launched into the boat, the boat was launched on to the sea. He sat on his mother's knee, gazing upon the white-bearded, blue-jerseyed fisherman (one of the very few men he could not possibly mistake for his father) plying the oars a couple of arm's lengths from him. He was invited by the kindly fisherman to come and stand between his knees as he rowed and he went and stood there, facing his mother, and his mother, rising to really fine heights, gave him an account of the marvels of the element on which he was now riding, the big and little fishes that lived and played and went to school therein, that would have fascinated, I believe, even Sir Isaac Newton himself. From that the boat and all its contents were as absorbingly described. "Look at the fisherman's 'normous big hands! Look at the oars that make the boat go along! Look at this funny thing, called an anchor! Look at this funny thing called a lobster pot! Look at all this heaps and heaps of string, called a fishing line! Look at, oh, just look at——"

"Don't like those bullocks on the road," said Simon.

## V

### *The Astounding Mind of My Son*

 HAVE written heretofore of my son Simon with a certain lightness; and with lightness no doubt he and all of his age (nearly three) should be regarded. Who takes a wheel to break a butterfly? But this time I am going to write of him, of his mind, of the marvel and the mystery of his astounding mind, with the thoughts that contemplation of that marvel and of that mystery often arouse in me; and I would say that they are not lightsome thoughts. They go too deep, or at all events they carry me too deeply, for prankishness.

Imagine at nearly three that mind of his! I imagine it, you know, as a little house, a little honeycomb, made up of pearly white cells—glistening, dewy, lustrous, semi-transparent, pearly, pearly white cells; untrodden, untouched, and pure—oh, pure beyond all conception of purity. Imagine by contrast with it the honeycomb house of a long-used mind, the mind of one past middle age, and you will realize how pure [74] and white and glistening and untouched it is.

Imagine the trodden, trampled, often miry foot-paths (no, thought paths) of a long-used mind, pitted with grievances, scarred with uglinesses, cumbered with useless lumber, strewn with out-worn hopes, clouded with disappointments and with sorrows, rusty with neglected opportunities, creaking with dismal, hopeless habits.

And then imagine the little lustrous honey-comb of cells of pearly, pearly white that my son Simon's is!

What is there in it? Who live there? Well, it is inhabited, this pearly honeycomb of my son Simon's, as far as I can make out, by a half dozen or so of amazing creatures, principally of the farmyard; and that is about all. There is a Moo goes wandering about this pearly honeycomb, and a Baa and a Gee and (to use my son Simon's pronunciation) a Piggyvig, and a Gooaat and a Man. There they live, these astounding creatures—astounding as my son Simon sees them, for there is nothing from talking upwards that they cannot do—and they are set in motion by stories told him by his mother and his father, and the pearly white brain cells coil and · twist and turn all over them as they move, causing [75] them to do things infinitely more amazing than any invention of his father or his mother possibly could contrive.

My son Simon, you see, is limited in understanding of all he hears by the very few words that he really does comprehend. He can repeat any word now (an amazing child!) but the vast majority that he repeats are entirely meaningless to him. His cot stands between our beds at night and always in the dim hours of the morning when adults desire nothing of life but sleep he raids one or the other and makes himself (speaking for my own part) an abominable nuisance. Sleepily and angrily passing him a toy when he had raided mine the other morning, I was not satisfied with his expression of thanks (I am very stern about his manners) and "Say 'Thank you' properly," I irritably commanded. "Thank you poperly," drowsily grunted my son Simon, snuggling with his toy into the small of my back. It is his delight to take the letters from the aged postman who brings them to us of a morning and, receiving them the other day, "Say 'Thank you', darling," he was called to by his [76] mother, tenderly watching. "Thank you, dar-

*"Thank you, darling,"* said my son Simon to the venerable postman.

ling," said my son Simon to the venerable postman.

Meaningless, you see, half the words that are entered into that pearly honeycomb that is his mind and projected out of the perfect bow of Cupid that is its gateway; and what I propose to talk about now is my apprehension of what goes on in that pearly honeycomb when the meaningless symbols come in, and how the pearly cells, entirely at loss, cling on to the few figures, the Moo and the Baa and the Piggyvig and the rest, that they know so well and are certain of. I tell him, you understand, the remarkable diversion of a Moo which I have seen in the course of a walk; and all he really comprehends is that this amazing Moo that lives in his pearly honeycomb is somehow mixed up in the business; and the pearly white cells churn round and round that Moo and produce for my son Simon goodness knows exactly what, but, enormously and all the time, that Moo. It is to that he clings.

In example, I passed the other day a herd of Moos being driven by a boy on a bicycle; and as this was a phenomenon it never yet had occurred to me to present to my son Simon I hurried home to tell him all about it; and told him; something like this:

"Dad was out for a vork."

Nearly all my son Simon's w's and v's and words, *vurds*, sound so much more delightful to me like that that, in conversation with my son Simon, I cannot resist pronouncing them so.

"Dad was out for a vork and in the road Dad saw a lot of Moos. A lot and a lot. Dad saw them. Red-faced Moos and black-faced Moos and vite-faced Moos. And, what do you think? There was no Man with them. There was a Boy with them. And, what do you think? The Boy with the Moos was not vorking with the Moos; he was riding a bicycle like Dad's bicycle with the Moos. Dad saw him. All the Moos were vorking along saying 'Moo—Moo!' and the Boy with them was not walking with them; he was riding a bicycle with them. Dad saw him. There! Wasn't that funny! What do you think of that?"

What does he think of it? If you could see his face while he has been listening to it you would know at least that he has been thinking with a concentration not surpassed (in its degree) by a judge assimilating the pleading of an intricate point of law by counsel, by student following the tortuous path leading him to heart of a problem expounded by professor. My son Simon, thinking—thinking of my Moos, of the Bicycle, of the Boy, of the Road, and of his Father watching the Moos, the Bicycle, the Boy and the Road—is presented by his face, by its deepened eyes, by the shadow of a pucker upon the ivory skin above the deepened eyes, as wrapt, plunged, buried and utterly entombed in thought. A graven image is not more inscrutable. The Court of Appeal about to give judgment is not more profound.

I have to arouse him; and it is by repeating my plea for his verdict—"There! Wasn't that funny? What do you think of that?"—that, I think, I will arouse him. It has been, in my opinion, a dashed fine real-life story. That Boy attending those Moos on that Bicycle instead of the normal monotonous man with a stick was a master touch, a most moving incident. I must know. I demand to know, how it strikes my son; so "There!" I cry again, "wasn't that funny? On a Bicycle! What do you think of that?"

He announces what he thinks. He gives his verdict. He pronounces his judgment.     [81]

Deep-toned, infinitely portentous, bowed down as it were with the enormous responsibility of the thing: "They were Moos," he adjudicates.

They were Moos! All my beautiful real-life story come out to simply that! They were Moos! "Great gosh, boy," I am inclined to cry, "of course they were Moos. Everybody knows that. Boy alive, that's not the point! The point isn't the blinking Moos. The point is that a Boy on a Bicycle—on a *Bicycle*, man—was driving the Moos. Great gosh, don't you ——"

But I do not cry these expostulations. I restrain myself. I realize what has been happening in that pearly honeycomb that is the mind of this my son, aged almost three years old. That astounding old Moo who lives there, familiar to him as his Dad himself, is, in all the churning up by all those pearly cells of all the figures that I have projected into them, the only thing that has remained solid, stolid, stable, enduring, calm, familiar, reassuring, consoling, comforting to my son Simon. Round and round the Bicycle the pearly cells have churned, round the Boy, round the Road, round the Moos on the Road, round

his Dad watching Boy, Bicycle and Moos on the

Road; and in the phantasmagoria of it all my son Simon has clung might and main on to that old Moo and come out of it as it were with his arms around its neck, rescued by it. "They were Moos," he announces, rescued.

For what do you suppose he has seen during my recital? What do you suppose those pearly cells of the glistening honeycomb of his mind to which everything is new have presented to him? They can present, mind you, nothing impossible because to those white untrodden cells everything is as possible and as natural as are the most outrageous impossibilities to you and me when we are dreaming. Phantasmagoria is the word I have used for what he has been watching while I have been telling; and phantasmagoria, that terrific word, is the right word. Phantasmagoria: "a crowd (says the dictionary) or succession of dim or doubtfully real figures"; and dim or doubtfully, fearfully real are the things that the pearly cells of my son Simon's mind have been showing him—the Boy, the Bicycle, the Moos, the Road, his Father. Probably the Moos on the Bicycle, the Boy on the Moos, the Road coiled all about the mass and his Father astound-

ingly and commandingly coiled all around the
Road. What a perplexity! What a night-
mare! What in wonder does it all mean?
What in wonder is he to make of it all?

"They were Moos," he makes; and I, what
do I do? Well, I give a crack or a break of
laughter and hug him to me.

I would, you see, that he might live for ever
just like that; never any older; never any wiser;
clinging in all the phantasmagoria that go whirling
through his pearly cells to that old Moo he knows
and trusts so well. Of course he cannot. Of
course he must grow up. Of course those pearly
cells must grow trodden, pitted, crowded, clouded,
vexed. Well, I wish for him, then, that, as he
grows and as the trials come, he may house in
those cells a Faith to which in his manhood he
can turn with all the certitude, the comfort, the
consolation, the reassurance with which now in
his babyhood he turns to that old Moo.

"They were Moos," says he, that tried old Moo
supporting him.

"I—'Hold we fall to rise, are baffled to fight
better, sleep to wake,' " I trust he will declare, his
Faith supporting him.

## *The Astounding Beauty of My Son*

THIS time, this record being in a manner of speaking my leave-taking of my son Simon, or in a better way of speaking my son Simon's leave-taking of his audience,—this time I propose to take my courage in my hands and, preparing for hasty flight, write quite brazenly of the beauty of my son.

It requires some courage. Every cow, as they say, thinks its own calf the finest; and every hen, as Mark Twain's Pudd'nhead Wilson said, when it has laid an egg cackles as loudly as if it had laid an asteroid, which is another way of saying the same thing; and every mother, white, brown or black, when she hears me daring to call my son Simon beautiful, will cry, *"That* child beautiful!"* and, outraged in her deepest depths, will snatch up from its cot, its cradle or its nursery and thrust forward at me——

Well, you know, I have had quite a multitude of infants thrust forward at me since my son Simon came; or rather I have thrust myself forward at them wherever in my goings to and [85] fro I have espied them; and I have peered at them keenly but generously, minutely but without prejudice, and, well, really, you know, they are not, they simply are not—well, I hate to hurt any one's feelings, especially a mother's, but they really are not beautiful at all, not as my son Simon is beautiful, really they are not.

Let us leave for a moment, tarrying the hasty flight that otherwise will be forced upon me, the beauty of his face and form; the perfect moulding, the exquisite material; the skin transparent almost in its delicacy, the astonishing fairness of his colouring shining beneath the glorious fairness of his hair—let us leave all that (which only makes you furious) and look down deeper, into, I mean, the lovely beauty of his mind, his character.

I bought him the other day a collection of farmyard animal models, positive little works of art in metal and only from a penny to tuppence each, pick 'em where you like. I picked two bobsworth and, trembling with excitement, hurried them home. My son Simon was just bedded up for the night and it was cruelty to children, I was told, to show them to him then. He could be

shown them simply to have them taken away

from him again immediately. He would never go to sleep. He would want them, and it would not be good for him to have them, and he would perhaps cry for them, and it would not be good for him to be unhappy as he fell asleep, and so on and so on.

Yes, but what about me? No one ever seems to think of me in these conditions. What about me? Was it good for me, did any one suppose, to have these perfectly enrapturing animals in my possession for my son Simon and not to be able to give them to my son Simon? Would *I* be able to sleep, did any one imagine, with these absolutely lifelike moos and baas and gees and piggyvigs on my mind, and with this tumultuous anticipation of the effect of these almost living animals on the mind of my son Simon? Would it be good for me, did any one conjecture, to lie awake all night imagining the raptures of my son and forced to await the dawn before I might arouse those raptures? Should I be able to work to-morrow if I got no rest to-night? No, no. Fathers must be considered as well as sons. Unhand me. Let me go.

And up I trod—no, leapt and bounded up. [87]

I am not describing the raptures. I have not the pen that could describe them. In so far as my son Simon's raptures were concerned with the moos, the baas and the gees, I doubt very much whether any pen exists that could describe them. In so far as his transports were concerned with the piggyvigs I am absolutely certain that there is no such pen. The piggyvigs ravished him. He concentrated on the piggyvigs, and the piggyvigs as it were ate him up and devoured him, mind, body and soul. He curled down to sleep ultimately with the whole world and all that therein is, himself included, solely and wholly and to the exclusion of all and everybody else a metal model piggyvig.

He curled, I say to sleep; contentedly to sleep; the whole séance, manifestation or revelation of the piggyvigs and the rest not having occupied above ten minutes, and the fears that he never would sleep again being triumphantly disproved in the eleventh minute—partly as some of his adorers would say because he is as good as he is beautiful; partly as I would say because he is as intelligent as he is beautiful; but mostly by a combination of these qualities arising out of the fact that I have a way with him, or rather that we have a way with one another, resultant on our mutual realisation that we are a couple of men alone together in a house of women and must comport ourselves like that—shoulder to shoulder, back to back; in a word, supporting one another, sympathising with one another and respecting one another.

What, in short, my son Simon and I say to one another goes; and the contract or Kellogg Pact between us is, up to the present, that in cases of difference of opinion or of judgment between us what I say goes furthest.

Well, I produce—taking back to the eighth or ninth minute the thread of my recital—I produce an empty cigarette box, likewise a clean handkerchief. With the handkerchief we lay a delicious bed on the floor of the box, on the delicious bed we compose to slumber, with suitable admonitions, the piggyvigs, the moos, the baas and the gees.

We close the box.

I place the box on the chest of drawers in line of vision from cot or beds.

"In the morning," I announced, "Simon [89]

will say, 'Please, Dad, I want that box,' and Dad will get the box and Dad will get a large book for a farmyard and make gee stables and piggyvig stables on it, and Simon and Dad will get out all the piggyvigs and all the aminals (his word) and play with them."

He is content. My son Simon is a signatory to the Man Pact between us and he knows that I am a signatory and that what we say to one another goes, and that, because we have said it, the piggyvigs in the morning will come. He is content. I snuggle him down. He lifts a last eye at the box bulging with piggyvigs. He closes a last eye upon a mind bulging with piggyvigs. I leave him. He sleeps.

And where, all this time, I hear mothers inquiring, each trembling ready with example of her own Simon's or Simon's lovely nature, is the wonderful beauty of character we were to be shown? Well, there has been a flicker of it, I suggest, not alone in the tractability that will give up a marvel without a murmur, but, lovelier far, in the assurance that will go to sleep in a world that is one rapturous piggyvig assured (because his parent says so) that it will wake to rapturous piggyvig again. It is, I often think, the most beautiful aspect of childhood—that implicit trust, that absolute belief, not so much in the word as in the omnipotence of a parent. There is nothing that, in its belief, its mother or its father cannot do; and that throws, I think, an enormous responsibility on to a parent—not in childhood's infancy but when, developing intelligence, it will be able to see (perhaps) that its idol has but feet of clay.

These are sombre thoughts, however; and the assurance of my son Simon that he would be restored on waking to a world one universal piggyvig is far from being the instance of his beauty of character which I propose to present.

That, in the morning's sequel to the night's events, comes now.

It would have been about six o'clock when I was aroused by his raiding of my bed and by his voice: "Want that box! Want that box!"

Dash that box! It was an odd thing with me but I find myself not nearly so—shall I say fatherly?—towards my son Simon at six in the morning as at six in the evening. At six in the evening when he is going to bed I am, so to speak, [91] all father, every fibre of me. At six in the morning when I am in my own bed I am, to the exclusion of all other emotions, all asleep, every bone, pulse, member and muscle of me.

"Want that box!"

He is not clamouring for it. He never clamours. He merely, in his soft, engaging little voice, is stating his desire: "Want that box!"

Dash that infernal box! The soft, engaging little voice, at six a.m., engages me nothing. Dash the box! and, dashing it, I grunt the password of our Pact for stipulation of delay. "Minute! Minute!" I grunt, and I clutch out with imploring hands at retreating sleep and I catch her (hog that I am) before she goes.

I awake to better consciousness. I do not know how long I have slept since my son Simon came in for his box. The morning certainly is lighter. He is lying at my back, perfectly quiet. Perhaps he is asleep; and I turn around to see.

He is not asleep. He is lying flat on his back, his eyes, wide open, directed on the chest of drawers where stands the box. My movement appears not to disturb him. Just like that he continues to lie, turns not even his eyes to me, and

*"Finking those piggyvigs in that box."*

I gaze a moment at that quite exquisite face which is the face that my son Simon has. . . .

Then, using the language that is his language and therefore, when we are together, mine, I address him:

"Vot you finking?"

Still he does not move his eyes from their direction. A smile so tiny, so delicate, so infinitely tender that, tempted to call it angelic, I find a better word for it in "secret"—a secret smile, privy to himself, intended in no way for me, divides his lips, and he murmurs out of it: "Finking those piggyvigs in that box."

Beauty of character! Will you not grant me beauty of character for my son Simon who can lie like that, eyes on his heart's desire, mind on his heart's desire, kept from his heart's desire only by his father hog-deep in swinish sleep, and quite content, until the hog emerges, just to lie "finking those piggyvigs in that box?"

I believe you will.

Or shall I drop beauty (only annoying you) and tell you instead some of the fun of his character arising out of the Male Pact between us, and how and why his character of the near future [95] will present him as a neat boy who keeps his hair short and parts it, not one of these shag-headed scrubs I see going about nowadays, and as a tidy boy who does not slop things about?

It is because, if I am to tell you, of what I called "Walloping-whacks" when I first (because he wanted to sit on instead of at the tea table), threatened him with these Child's Guides to Knowledge and what he (and therefore I) have since called "Valloping-vacks." They are, in my opinion, a good wholesome article to have about a house containing children, and they are now in daily use between my son Simon and I; but it is I, not he, who receives them; he, not I, who administers them—to his unbounded delight.

The thing is done on the principle of those unfortunate whipping-boys who in mediæval times were attached to the persons of young princes. It was not good, it was then held, that a prince should be chastised; and a prince therefore, erring and deserving to be chastised, was chastised on the person of his whipping-boy, and was supposed, by remorse at the other's suffering, to correct and refrain from the practises that had caused it.

I am my son Simon's whipping-boy.

Every morning when I make my early tea, my son Simon, at the critical moment when, on my knees, I lift the brimming, boiling can from the gas ring and transfer its contents into the teapot, peers down upon me tiptoe over the railing of his cot, trembling with delicious anticipation of my spilling some.

I always spill some.

Immediately and not a moment before, "Naughty Dad spill the vorter, volloping-vack!" bawls my son Simon, wild with glee; and I stretch up my devoted head and receive upon it down over the rail of the cot a stupendous volloping-vack that might, *might*, disturb a butterfly, so soft his tiny hand is; and I fill the air with my lamentations and with my protests that never again will I spill the vorter; and my son Simon hops and leaps with glee—and the idea is that in years to come, this most beneficial object lesson unconsciously sunken into him, he may, *may*, be tidy and not slop things about.

So with my hair. There should be, my son [97]

Simon knows, a parting in my hair; and whenever I am conscious that there is not a parting in my hair I go to my son Simon and, without a word, present my head to him—and he realises in a bound the full zest and snap of the joy of life.

"Naughty Dad no parting, volloping-vack!" shouts my son Simon; and again the mighty blow, again the possible annoyance to a butterfly had one been there, again the cries and promises for the future of a full-grown father suffering that his son, in years to come, may have the instinct for keeping his head well-groomed.

Well, no, I daresay that is only my fun. I daresay these performances are only done for my delight and for the delight of my son Simon. I daresay that I will leave his neatness and his tidyness to chance and will prefer to try to teach him (as his best gift in life) his mother's priceless gift of laughing not *at* a joke but *with* a joke: a difference which you will perhaps appreciate when I put it as the difference between the shrill unkind bray of laughter which some characters will give at a ludicrous object and the quite dif-

ferent laughter that my wife will give—softened

with sympathy, touched with a lovely tenderness of compassion: laughing *with*, not laughing *at*.

I think I will just hope that for your beauty of character, Simon, old boy; and for memory of your beauty of form and face as you now are I just will remember all my life, secret to myself as that smile of yours while you lay finking the piggy-vigs in that box was secret, just that exquisite caress of your small hand upon my head that you call volloping-vack.

So long, old boy, so long!

CPSIA information can be obtained at www.ICGtesting.com
Printed in the USA
BVOW04s0020030215

386108BV00020B/214/P